A Crash Course in the Bible

Larry Vaughn

Copyright ©2018 by Larry Vaughn

All rights reserved. No part of this book may be reproduced in any form or by any electronic or mechanical means including information storage and retrieval systems without permission in writing from the publisher, except by a reviewer, who may quote brief passages in a review.

All Scripture quotations, unless otherwise indicated, are taken from the King James Version.

Scripture quotations marked ESV are taken from the ESV® Bible (The Holy Bible, English Standard Version®), copyright ©2001 by Crossway, a publishing ministry of Good News Publishers. Used by permission. All rights reserved.

Scripture quotations marked NCV are taken from the New Century Version®, copyright ©2005 by Thomas Nelson. Used by permission. All rights reserved.

Dedication

To my grandchildren:

Michael, Jason, Sarah, Jacob, Adam, Haley, Beverly, Katie, John, Connor and Spencer.

And my great-grandchildren:

Lillyanne, Lennon and Jase

Contents

Introduction 3
The Blessing of the Lord 11
The Blood of Jesus 15
Children 19
Commandments 21
Correction 27
The Desires of Your Heart 31
Eternal Life 34
The Faith 37
Forgiveness of Sins 39
God's Help 41
God's Rest 44
Heaven 47
The Holy Spirit 50
Inheritance 53
Judgment 56
Justification 59
The Kingdom of God 62
The Lamb of God 66

The Law	68
The Living Word of God	71
Marriage	73
The New Birth	77
The New Covenant	80
Our High Priest	84
Recompense	86
Redemption	88
The Righteousness of Christ	90
Salvation	93
Sonship	96
The Spirit of Truth	100
Spiritual Bread	103
Spiritual Drink	107
Spiritual Meat	110
The Voice of God	112
The Will of God	116
Wisdom	119
The Written Word of God	122
Your Personal Savior	126
12 Things You Need to Know	128

Introduction

If you had gone to public school fifty years ago, you would have learned the true history of the United States. You would have learned that we come from a long line of people who loved God, loved their country and based their lives on the Bible. And you would have learned that the freedom and prosperity we enjoy were given to us by God.

Noah Webster is called "The Father of American Scholarship and Education." In his *American Dictionary of the English Language*, he said: "Every civil government is based upon some religion or philosophy of life. Education in a nation will propagate the religion of that nation. In America, the foundational religion was Christianity. And it was sown in the hearts of Americans through the home and private and public schools for centuries.

Our liberty, growth, and prosperity was the result of a Biblical philosophy of life. Our continued freedom and success is dependent on our educating the youth of America in the principles of Christianity."

The Supreme Court destroyed our education system in 1963, when they made it illegal to teach the Bible in public schools. And in 1990, when they made it illegal to post the Ten Commandments in public schools.

These are the same Ten Commandments that God gave to Moses on Mt. Sinai. The same Ten Commandments on which our entire justice system is built. And the same Ten Commandments which have defined our culture for centuries.

Millions of Americans believe that the Bible is the word of God. But they have no idea what's in it because nobody's ever taught it to them. If they want to know what the Bible says, they'll have to learn it on their own.

And that's where *A Crash Course in the Bible* comes in handy. It contains essential Bible verses that everyone needs to know. They're in a topical index. And they're accompanied by notes that explain their meaning.

A Crash Course in the Bible gives you a large amount of valuable information from the Bible. And you can learn it in a very short time. Then, you'll have a working knowledge of the Bible. And you can base your life on it and teach it to your children.

That's the formula for living a long and happy life: learn the Bible, base your life on it and to teach it to your children. Learn it. Live it. Teach it.

It's impossible for us to earn our own salvation. So God gives it to us by grace. Grace is the unmerited favor of God. **"For by grace are ye saved through faith; and that not of yourselves: it is the gift of God: not of works, lest any man should boast." (Ephesians 2:8-9)**

We receive God's free gift of salvation through faith in his word. **"Therefore it is of faith, that it might be by grace, to the end the promise might be sure to all the seed; not to that only which is of the law, but to that also which is of the faith of Abraham; who is the father of us all." (Romans 4:16)**

Abraham believed that God's word is true. And God counted his faith as righteousness. If you believe that God's word is true, then God counts your faith as righteousness too. **"He staggered not at the promise of God through unbelief, but was strong in faith, giving glory to God; and being fully persuaded that, what he has promised, he was also able to perform. And therefore it was imputed to him for righteousness.**

Now it was not written for his sake alone, that it was imputed to him; but for us also, to whom it shall be imputed, if we believe on him that raised up Jesus our Lord from the dead. Who was delivered for our offenses, and was raised again for our justification." (Romans 4:20-24)

You don't have to do anything to earn your salvation. **"Not by works of righteousness which we have done, but according to his mercy he saved us, by the washing of regeneration, and renewing of the Holy Spirit." (Titus 3:5)**

When you put your faith in Jesus, he puts his Spirit in you and gives you spiritual life. Then, you're living by faith in Jesus Christ. And you can truthfully say, **"I am crucified with Christ: nevertheless I live; yet not I, but Christ liveth in me; and the life which I now live in the flesh I live by the faith of the Son of God, who loved me and gave his life for me." (Galatians 2:20)**

There are many people in the Christian community who think they're Christians when they're not. They're Christians in name only, because they don't have the Holy Spirit living in them. The Bible says, **"Now if any man have not the Spirit of God, he is none of his." (Romans 8:9)**

The parable of the ten virgins appears in Matthew Chapter Twenty-five. In this parable, the ten virgins represent the Christian community. Their lamps represent their hearts. The Bridegroom represents Jesus. And the oil represents the Holy Spirit, who lives in the hearts of everyone who belongs to Jesus.

The wise virgins have the Holy Spirit and the foolish virgins don't. And the Lord tells the foolish virgins, **"Truly I say to you, I do not know you." (Matthew 25:12 ESV)** The meaning of this parable is clear. If the Holy Spirit lives in you, you're on the way to Heaven. And if he doesn't, you're on the way to Hell.

You know that the Spirit of Christ lives in you when you're keeping the Lord's commandments. **"And hereby we do know that we know him, if we keep his commandments. He that saith, I**

know him, and keepeth not his commandments is a liar, and the truth is not in him. But whoso keepeth his word, in him verily is the love of God perfected: hereby know we that we are in him." (1 John 2:3-5)

Merely believing that God exists, or that Jesus exists, is not enough to save you. **"Thou believest that there is one God; thou doest well. The demons also believe and tremble."** (James 2:19)

To be saved, you must believe what the Bible says about Jesus---that he died for your sins and that God raised him from the dead. And you have to make a confession of faith in him that comes from your heart.

"The word is nigh thee, even in thy mouth, that is the word of faith which we preach; that if thou confess with thy mouth the Lord Jesus, and shalt believe in thine heart that God hath raised him from the dead, thou shalt be saved. For with the heart man believeth unto righteousness; and with the mouth confession is made unto salvation." (Romans 10:8-10)

Jesus is God's greatest gift. And we receive all of God's other gifts through him. The Bible says, **"He that spareth not his own Son, but delivered him up for us all, how shall he not with him also freely give us all things."** (**Romans 8:32**) And it also says that God gives us **"all things that pertain to life and godliness." (2 Peter 1:3)**

This book describes thirty-eight of God's gifts and it also tells you how to receive them. **"Now we have received, not the spirit of the world, but the spirit which is of God; that we might know the things that are freely given to us of God." (1 Corinthians 2:12)**

One of the best of these gifts is the blessing of the Lord.

The Blessing of the Lord

God promised us that if we keep his commandments, he will bless us. And that promise is still in effect because God's word is true and it lasts forever. **"The grass withereth, the flower fadeth: but the word of our God shall stand forever." (Isaiah 40:8)** The blessing of the Lord applies to us both as individuals and as a nation.

The following passage describes the blessing of the Lord: **"And if you faithfully obey the voice of the Lord your God, being careful to do all his commandments that I command you today, the Lord your God will set you high above all the nations of the earth. And all these blessings shall come upon you and overtake you, if you obey the voice of the Lord your God.**

Blessed shall you be in the city and blessed shall you be in the field. Blessed shall be the

fruit of your womb and the fruit of your ground and the fruit of your cattle, the increase of your herds and the young of your flock. Blessed shall be your basket and your kneading bowl. Blessed shall you be when you come in, and blessed shall you be when you go out.

The Lord will cause your enemies who rise against you to be defeated before you. They shall come out against you one way and flee before you seven ways. The Lord will command the blessing on you in your barns and in all that you undertake. And he will bless you in the land that the Lord your God is giving you. The Lord will establish you as a people holy unto himself, as he hath sworn to you, if you keep the commandments of the Lord and walk in his ways.

And all the peoples of the earth shall see that you are called by the name of the Lord, and they shall be afraid of you. And the Lord will make you abound in prosperity, in the fruit of your womb and in the fruit of your livestock and in the fruit of your ground,

within the land that the Lord swore to your fathers to give you.

The Lord will open to you his good treasure, the heavens, to give the rain to your land in its season and to bless all the work of your hands. And you shall lend to many nations, but you shall not borrow. And the Lord will make you the head and not the tail, and you shall only go up and not down, if you obey the commandments of the Lord your God, which I command you today, being careful to do them, and if you do not turn aside from any of the words that I command you today, to the right hand or to the left, to go after other gods to serve them." (Deuteronomy 28:1-14 ESV)

God's blessing makes us rich in every sense of the word. And the riches that God provides won't bring us any sorrow. **"The blessing of the Lord, it maketh rich, and he addeth no sorrow with it." (Proverbs 10:22)**

These are the requirements for receiving God's blessing. **"He that hath clean hands, and** a pure heart; who hath not lifted up his soul unto vanity, nor sworn deceitfully, He shall receive the blessing from the Lord, and righteousness from the God of his salvation." (Psalm 24:4-5)

If you fear the Lord, he will bless you. And he will bless your children too. **"He will bless them that fear the Lord, both small and great. The Lord shall increase you more and more, you and your children. Ye are blessed of the Lord which made heaven and earth. The heaven, even the heavens, are the Lord's: but the earth hath he given to the children of men." (Psalm 115:13-16)**

The Blood of Jesus

When the Israelites were slaves in Egypt, God sent Moses to deliver them. When Pharaoh refused to let them go, God sent ten plagues against Egypt. The last of these plagues was the death of the firstborn. And God made a way for his people to escape from it. He had them apply lamb's blood to the doorposts of their houses. And when the Death Angel saw the blood, he passed over them. The lamb's blood was a symbol for the blood of Jesus. And the blood of Jesus saves you from death when you apply it to the doorposts of your heart.

The Jewish feast of Passover is a celebration of that original "passover." The Last Supper is the Passover meal that Jesus attended on the night he was betrayed. That's where he established the Lord's Supper as an ordinance of the church. The bread and the wine of the Lord's Supper are symbols of the New Covenant. The bread represents Jesus' body, which was broken for us. And the wine represents his blood, which was shed for us.

Jesus told his disciples, **"For this is the blood of the new testament, which is shed for many for the remission of sins."** (Matthew 26:28) And the Bible tells us, **"Without the shedding of blood there is no remission of sin."** (Hebrews 9:22)

The blood of Jesus is the only sacrifice for sin that God accepts. And it applies to everyone who belongs to Jesus. **"How much more shall the blood of Christ, who through the eternal Spirit offered himself without spot to God, purge your own conscience from dead works to serve the living God? And for this cause he is the mediator of the new testament, that by means of death, for the redemption of the transgressions that were under the first testament, they which are called might receive the promise of eternal inheritance."** (Hebrews 9:14-15)

When you're in Christ, you're in right-standing with God. And when you walk in the light of God's word, you're in fellowship with God. **"This then is the message which we have heard of him, and declare unto you, that God is light, and in him is no darkness at all. If we say that we have fellowship with him, and walk in darkness, we lie, and do not the truth: But if we walk in the light, as he is in the light, we have fellowship one with another, and the blood of Jesus Christ his Son cleanseth us from all sin." (1 John 1:5-7)**

In this passage, Paul is speaking to Gentile believers in Jesus. Under the Old Covenant, we had no access to God. But he made us part of the New Covenant. **"That at that time ye were without Christ, being aliens from the commonwealth of Israel, and strangers from the covenants of promise, having no hope, and without God in the world: But now, in Christ Jesus ye who sometimes were far off are made nigh by the blood of Christ." (Ephesians 2:12-13)**

You are not your own. You've been bought with a price. That price is the blood of Jesus. And it covers all of your sins. So when God looks at you, he doesn't see your sins. He sees the blood of his own dear Son. Atonement is payment for a debt that is owed. **"For the life of the flesh is in the blood: and I have given it to you upon the altar to make an atonement for your souls: for it is the blood that maketh an atonement for the soul." (Leviticus 17:11)**

Children

Every child is a precious gift from God. **"As arrows are in the hand of a mighty man; so are children of the youth. Happy is the man that hath his quiver full of them: they shall not be ashamed, but they shall speak with the enemies in the gate." (Psalm 127:3-5)**

If you teach your children to walk in God's ways, they will walk in them for life. As the twig is bent, so grows the tree. **"Train up a child in the way he should go: and when he is old, he will not depart from it." (Proverbs 22:6)**

If your children walk in God's ways, they will have great peace. **"And all thy children shall be taught of the Lord; and great shall be the peace of thy children." (Isaiah 54:13)**

When we're adults, we have to stop thinking and acting like children. **"When I was a child, I** spake as a child, I understood as a child, I thought as a child: but when I became a man, I put away childish things." (1 Corinthians 13:11)

Fathers, don't turn your children into angry young people. Teach them how to walk in God's ways. **"And, ye fathers, provoke not your children to wrath: but bring them up in the nurture and admonition of the Lord." (Ephesians 6:4)**

Commandments

This is what God said about his people. "**O that there were such a heart in them, that they would fear me, and keep all my commandments always, that it might be well with them, and with their children forever!**" **(Deuteronomy 5:29)**

These are the Ten Commandments which God gave to Moses on Mt Sinai: "**And God spake all these words, saying, I am the L**ORD **thy God, which have brought thee out of the land of Egypt, out of the house of bondage.**

Thou shalt have no other gods before me. Thou shalt not make unto thee any graven image, or any likeness of any thing that is in heaven above, or that is in the earth beneath, or that is in the water under the earth.

Thou shalt not bow down thyself to them, nor serve them: for I the L<small>ORD</small> **thy God am a jealous God, visiting the iniquity of the fathers upon the children unto the third and fourth generation of them that hate me; And shewing mercy unto thousands of them that love me, and keep my commandments.**

Thou shalt not take the name of the L<small>ORD</small> **thy God in vain; for the** L<small>ORD</small> **will not hold him guiltless that taketh his name in vain.**

Remember the sabbath day, to keep it holy. Six days shalt thou labour, and do all thy work: But the seventh day is the sabbath of the L<small>ORD</small> **thy God: in it thou shalt not do any work, thou, nor thy son, nor thy daughter, thy manservant, nor thy maidservant, nor thy cattle, nor thy stranger that is within thy gates: For in six days the** L<small>ORD</small> **made heaven and earth, the sea, and all that in them is, and rested the seventh day: wherefore the** L<small>ORD</small> **blessed the sabbath day, and hallowed it.**

Honour thy father and thy mother: that thy days may be long upon the land which the LORD thy God giveth thee.

Thou shalt not kill. Thou shalt not commit adultery. Thou shalt not steal. Thou shalt not bear false witness against thy neighbour.

Thou shalt not covet thy neighbour's house, thou shalt not covet thy neighbour's wife, nor his manservant, nor his maidservant, nor his ox, nor his ass, nor any thing that is thy neighbour's." (Exodus 20:1-17)

This is what God said to his people: **"Come ye near unto me, hear ye this; I have not spoken in secret from the beginning; from the time that it was, there am I: and now the Lord God, and his Spirit, hath sent me. Thus saith the Lord, thy Redeemer, the Holy One of Israel; I am the Lord thy God which teacheth thee to profit, which leadeth thee by the way that thou shouldest go.**

O that thou hadst hearkened to my commandments! Then had thy peace been as a river, and thy righteousness as the waves of the sea:" (Isaiah 48:16-18)

When a lawyer asked Jesus about the law, Jesus told him that all of the law is based on two of God's commandments. **"Master, which is the great commandment in the law? Jesus said unto him, Thou shalt love the Lord thy God with all thy heart, and with all thy soul, and with all thy mind.**

This is the first and great commandment. And the second is like unto it, Thou shalt love thy neighbor as thyself. On these two commandments hang all the law and the prophets." (Matthew 22:36-40)

The Ten Commandments are based on two concepts---loving God and loving your neighbor. Loving God means doing his will. And loving your neighbor means doing him no harm. Jesus incorporated both of these ideas into a single commandment. **"A new Commandment I give**

unto you, That ye love one another; As I have loved you, that ye also love one another. By this shall all men know that ye are my disciples, if ye have love one to another." (John 13:34-35)

Jesus didn't do away with the Ten Commandments. He fulfilled them. And when you're keeping his commandment to love your neighbor, you're fulfilling them too. The Apostle Paul explained it like this:

"Owe no man anything, but to love one another: for he that loveth another hath fulfilled the law. For this, Thou shalt not commit adultery, Thou shalt not kill, Thou shalt not steal, Thou shalt not bear false witness, Thou shalt not covet; and if there be any other commandment, it is briefly comprehended in this saying, namely, Thou shalt love thy neighbor as thyself. Love worketh no ill to his neighbor: therefore love is the fulfilling of the law." (Romans 13:8-10)

God wants us to do two things: to believe on the name of his Son Jesus and to keep Jesus' commandment to love one other. **"And this is his commandment, That we should believe on the name of his Son Jesus Christ, and love one another, as he gave us commandment."** (1 John 3:23)

Jesus said, **"Those who know my commandments and obey them are the ones who love me and my Father will love those who love me. I will love them and will show myself to them."** (John 14:21 NCV)

If you keep God's commandments, then you will live a long, peaceful life. **"My son, forget not my law; but let thine heart keep my commandments: For length of days, and long life, and peace, shall they add to thee."** (Proverbs 3:1-2)

Correction

The Lord shows us what we're supposed to do. And we have to decide whether we'll do it or not. **"I will instruct thee and teach thee in the way which thou shalt go: I will guide thee with mine eye. Be ye not as the horse, or as the mule, which have no understanding; whose mouth must be held in with bit and bridle." (Psalm 32:8-9)**

Disciplining children is a big part of loving them. And the rod of correction is more figurative than it is literal. **"Whoever spares the rod hates his son, but he who loves him is diligent to discipline him." (Proverbs 13:24 ESV)**

Our God is an excellent Father. He rewards us when we obey him. And he corrects us when we don't. **"The Lord rewarded me because I did** what was right, because I did what the Lord said was right." (Psalm 18:24 NCV)

When the Lord corrects you, he's expressing his love for you. **"My son, despise not the chastening of the Lord; neither be weary of his correction: For whom the Lord loveth he correcteth; even as a father the son in whom he delighteth." (Proverbs 3:11-12)**

When the Lord corrects you, it proves that you belong to him. **"Thou shalt also consider in thine heart, that, as a man chasteneth his son, so the Lord thy God chasteneth thee." (Deuteronomy 8:5)**

The Lord's correction is very gentle. He nudges us into doing what's right. **"And thine ears shall hear a word behind thee, saying, this is the way, walk ye in it, when ye turn to the right hand, and when ye turn to the left." (Isaiah 30:21)**

God doesn't kick us out of his family when we sin. But he does correct us for it. **"If his children** forsake my law, and walk not in my judgments; If they break my statutes, and keep not my commandments; Then will I visit their transgression with the rod, and their iniquity with stripes. Nevertheless my loving-kindness will I not utterly take from him, nor suffer my faithfulness to fail. My covenant will I not break, nor alter the thing that is gone out of my lips." (Psalm 89:30-33)

Every sin has a built-in penalty. **"Thine own wickedness shall correct thee, and thy backslidings shall reprove thee: know therefore and see that it is an evil thing and bitter, that thou hast forsaken the Lord thy God, and that my fear is not in thee, saith the Lord God of hosts." (Jeremiah 2:19)**

So when we sin, it always costs us something. **"Your sins have withholden good things from you." (Jeremiah 5:25)**

If a man isn't rich toward God, then he isn't rich at all. Repenting is turning away from sin. **"Because thou sayest, I am rich, and** increased with goods, and have need of nothing; and knowest not that thou art wretched, and miserable, and poor, and blind, and naked: I counsel thee to buy of me gold tried in the fire, that thou mayest be rich; and white raiment, that thou mayest be clothed, and that the shame of thy nakedness do not appear; and anoint thine eyes with eyesalve, that thou mayest see. As many as I love, I rebuke and chasten: be zealous therefore, and repent." (Revelation 3:17-19)

The Desires of Your Heart

The Bible says to let your requests be made known unto God. It says that you have not because you ask not. And it also says, if you delight yourself in the Lord, he will give you the desires of your heart.

The Lord wants you to delight in him, to commit your way to him and to trust in him. **"Delight thyself also in the Lord; and he shall give thee the desires of thine heart. Commit thy way unto the Lord; trust also in him; and he shall bring it to pass. And he shall bring forth thy righteousness as the light, and thy judgment as the noonday." (Psalm 37:4-6)**

Delighting in the Lord is taking pleasure in doing his will. When your will and God's will are the same, then he will grant your requests. **"And this is the confidence that we have in him, that** if we ask any thing according to his will, he heareth us; And if we know that he hear us, whatever we ask, we know that we have the petitions that we desired of him." (1 John 5:14-15)

If you fear the Lord, then he will fulfill your desires. **"The Lord is righteous in all his ways, and holy in all his works. The Lord is nigh unto all them that call upon him, to all that call upon him in truth. He will fulfill the desire of them that fear him: he also will hear their cry, and will save them. The Lord preserveth all them that love him: but all the wicked will he destroy. My mouth shall speak the praise of the Lord: and let all flesh bless his holy name for ever and ever." (Psalm 145:17-21)**

Fear causes bad things to happen. And faith in God causes good things to happen. **"The fear of the wicked, it shall come upon him: but the desire of the righteous shall be granted." (Proverbs 10:24)**

When bad things happened to Job, he said, **"For the thing which I greatly feared is come upon me, and that which I was afraid of is come unto me." (Job 3:25)**

The righteous expect to receive good things from God. But the wicked expect God to punish them. **"The desire of the righteous is only good: but the expectation of the wicked is wrath." (Proverbs 12:23)**

This verse confirms the fact that God gives us the desires of our hearts. **"Thou hast given him his heart's desire, and hast not withholden the request of his lips. Selah." (Psalm 21:2)**

Eternal Life

Eternal life is a free gift from God. You don't have to do anything to earn it or deserve it. **"For the wages of sin is death; but the gift of God is eternal life through Jesus Christ our Lord." (Romans 6:23)**

This is Jesus' definition of eternal life: **"And this is eternal life, that they know you the only true God, and Jesus Christ whom you have sent." (John 17:3 ESV)**

Nicodemus was a religious leader who came to learn from Jesus. And Jesus told him how to obtain eternal life. **"And as Moses lifted up the serpent in the wilderness, even so must the Son of man be lifted up: That whosoever believeth in him should not perish, but have eternal life. For God so loved the world, that he gave his** only begotten Son, that whosoever believeth in him should not perish, but have everlasting life." (John 3:14-16)

The whole Bible is about Jesus. He is the source of eternal life. He said, **"Search the scriptures: for in them ye think ye have eternal life: and they are they which testify of me." (John 5:39)**

The Bible is the testimony of God. Anyone who denies that it's true is making God out to be a liar. **"If we receive the witness of men, the witness of God is greater: for this is the witness of God which he hath testified of his Son.**

He that believeth on the Son of God hath the witness in himself: he that believeth not God hath made him a liar; because he believeth not the record that God gave of his Son.

And this is the record, that God hath given to us eternal life, and this life is in his Son. He that hath the Son hath life; and he that hath

not the Son hath not life. These things have I written unto you that believe on the name of the Son of God; that ye may know that ye have eternal life, and that ye may believe on the name of the Son of God." (1 John 5:11-13)

The Faith

Being in the faith is knowing God's word and basing your life on it. **"But continue thou in the things which thou hast learned and hast been assured of, knowing of whom thou hast learned them; and that from a child thou hast known the holy scriptures, which are able to make thee wise unto salvation through faith which is in Christ Jesus.**

All scripture is given by inspiration of God, and is profitable for doctrine, for reproof, for correction, for instruction in righteousness: that the man of God may be perfect, thoroughly furnished unto all good works." (2 Timothy 3:14-17)

Departing from the faith is abandoning the truth of God's word and believing the Devil's lies instead. **"Now the Spirit speaketh expressly,**

that in the latter times some shall depart from the faith, giving heed to seducing spirits, and doctrines of devils;" (1 Timothy 4:1)

The fruit of the Holy Spirit is love, joy, peace, patience, kindness, goodness, faithfulness, gentleness, and self-control. If you're bearing these fruits, you know that Jesus is living in you. And you know that you're in the faith.

"Examine yourselves, to see whether you are in the faith. Test yourselves. Or do you not realize this about yourselves, that Jesus Christ is in you---unless indeed you fail to meet the test!" (2 Corinthians 13:5 ESV)

If a man doesn't provide for his own family, then he reveals the fact that he's not in the faith. **"But if any provide not for his own, and specially for those of his own house, he hath denied the faith, and is worse than an infidel." (1 Timothy 5:8)**

Forgiveness of Sins

The Prophet Micah prophesied that God would forgive our sins and not count them against us. **"Who is a God like unto thee, that pardoneth iniquity, and passeth by the transgression of the remnant of his heritage? He retaineth not his anger for ever, because he delighteth in mercy. He will turn again, he will have compassion upon us; he will subdue our iniquities; and thou wilt cast all their sins into the depths of the sea."** (Micah 7:18-19)

If you're in Christ, then God has forgiven all of your sins. **"The Lord is merciful and gracious, slow to anger, and plenteous in mercy. He will not always chide: neither will he keep his anger for ever. He hath not dealt with us after our sins; nor rewarded us according to our iniquities. For as the heaven is high above the earth, so great is his mercy toward them** that fear him. As far as the east is from the west, so far hath he removed our transgressions from us." (Psalm 103:8-12)

If you confess your sins to God, he will forgive them. And he will also cleanse you from all unrighteousness. **"If we say that we have no sin, we deceive ourselves, and the truth is not in us. If we confess our sins, he is faithful and just to forgive us our sins, and to cleanse us from all unrighteousness."** (1 John 1:8-9)

Not only does God forgive our sins, he also forgets about them. **"I, even I, am he that blotteth out thy transgressions for mine own sake, and will not remember thy sins."** (Isaiah 43:25)

It doesn't matter how bad your sins are, God will forgive them all. **"Come now, and let us reason together, saith the Lord: though your sins be as scarlet, they shall be white as snow; though they be red like crimson, they shall be as wool."** (Isaiah 1:18)

God's Help

God helps everyone whose heart is perfect toward him. **"For the eyes of the Lord run to and fro throughout the whole earth, to show himself strong in the behalf of them whose heart is perfect toward him." (2 Chronicles 16:9)**

Asa was the King of Judah and his heart was perfect toward God. When a vast army of Ethiopians was coming to destroy Judah, Asa asked God to help them. **"And Asa cried unto the Lord his God, and said, Lord, it is nothing with thee to help, whether with many, or with them that have no power: help us, O Lord our God; for we rest on thee, and in thy name we go against this multitude. O Lord, thou art our God; let not man prevail against thee." (2 Chronicles 14:11)**

God answered Asa's prayer and he destroyed the Ethiopian army. **"So the Lord smote the Ethiopians before Asa, and before Judah; and the Ethiopians fled. And Asa and the people that were with him pursued them unto Gerar: and the Ethiopians were overthrown, that they could not recover themselves; for they were destroyed before the Lord, and before his host; and they carried away very much spoil."** (2 Chronicles 14:12-13)

Don't be afraid of anybody or anything, because the Lord is always with you and he will help you. **"Fear thou not; for I am with thee: be not dismayed; for I am thy God: I will strengthen thee; Yea, I will help thee; yea, I will uphold thee with the right hand of my righteousness. . . . For I the Lord will hold thy right hand, saying unto thee, fear not; I will help thee."** (Isaiah 41:10, 13)

When you're good, the Lord directs your steps. And he keeps you from going down the drain. **"The steps of a good man are ordered by the Lord: and he delighted in his way. Though**

he fall, he shall not be utterly cast down: for the Lord upholdeth him with his hand." (Psalm 37:23-24)

When you're in trouble, cry out to God and he will help you. **"Call upon me in the day of trouble: I will deliver thee, and thou shalt glorify me." (Psalm 50:15)**

God's Rest

When God finished creating the heavens and the earth, he rested. Because there was nothing left for him to do. **"Thus the heavens and the earth were finished, and all the host of them. And on the seventh day God ended his work which he had made; and he rested on the seventh day from all his work which he had made. And God blessed the seventh day, and sanctified it: because that in it he had rested from all his work which God created and made." (Genesis 2:1-3)**

We are yoked together with Jesus. Everything we do is a joint-venture with him. And he does all of the heavy lifting. He says, **"Come unto me, all ye that labor and are heavy laden, and I will give you rest. Take my yoke upon you, and learn of me, for I am meek and lowly in heart: and ye shall find rest unto your souls. For my** yoke is easy, and my burden is light." (Matthew 11:28-30)

We have to learn God's ways in order to enter his rest. **"Whom shall he teach knowledge? And whom shall he make to understand doctrine? them that are weaned from the milk, and drawn from the breasts.**

For precept must be upon precept, precept upon precept; line upon line, line upon line; here a little, and there a little: for with stammering lips and another tongue will he speak to this people. To whom he said, This is the rest wherewith ye may cause the weary to rest; and this is the refreshing: yet they would not hear." (Isaiah 28: 9-12)

We have to walk in God's ways in order to enter his rest. **"Thus saith the Lord, Stand ye in the ways, and see, and ask for the old paths, where is the good way, and walk therein, and ye shall find rest for your souls. But they said, We will not walk therein. Also I set watchmen** over you, saying, Hearken to the sound of the trumpet. But they said, We will not hearken.

Therefore hear, ye nations, and know, O congregation, what is among them. Hear, O earth; behold, I will bring evil upon this people, even the fruit of their thoughts, because they have not hearkened unto my words, nor to my law, but rejected it." (Jeremiah 6:16-19)

Heaven

Jesus calls Heaven his Father's house. And he's preparing a place for you there. **"Let not your heart be troubled: ye believe in God, believe also in me. In my Father's house are many mansions: if it were not so, I would have told you. I go to prepare a place for you. And if I go and prepare a place for you, I will come again, and receive you unto myself; that where I am, there ye may be also." (John 14:1-3)**

Job lived centuries before Jesus was born. Yet he knew that he had a Redeemer. He said, **"For I know that my redeemer liveth, and that he shall stand at the latter day upon the earth:" (Job 19:25)** And Job also said, **"For I know that thou wilt bring me to death, and to the house appointed for all living." (Job 30:23)**

You are a spirit. You have a soul and you live in a body. Your soul consists of your mind, your emotions and your will. When you die, your spirit and your soul will immediately go to Heaven, where you will live with the Lord forever.

"Therefore we are always confident, knowing that whilst we are at home in the body, we are absent from the Lord: (For we walk by faith, not by sight:) We are confident, I say, and willing rather to be absent from the body, and to be present with the Lord." (2 Corinthians 5:6-9)

Shortly before he was crucified, Jesus prayed this prayer for us. **"Neither pray I for these alone, but for them also which shall believe on me through their word; . . . Father, I will that they also, whom thou hast given me, be with me where I am." (John 17:20, 24)**

Jesus was crucified between two thieves. And this is the record of what those three men said to each other. At that time, "Paradise," or "Abraham's Bosom," was the place of the righteous dead. **"And one of the malefactors which were hanged railed on him, saying, If thou be Christ, save thyself and us. But the other answering rebuked him, saying, Dost not thou fear God, seeing thou art in the same condemnation? And we indeed justly; for we receive the due reward of our deeds: but this man hath done nothing amiss. And he said unto Jesus, Lord, remember me when thou comest into thy kingdom. And Jesus said unto him, Verily I say unto thee, Today shalt thou be with me in paradise." (Luke 23:39-43)**

This verse gives us a glimpse of what our lives will be like in Heaven. **"And God shall wipe away all tears from their eyes; and there shall be no more death, neither sorrow, nor crying, neither shall there be any more pain: for the former things are passed away." (Revelation 21:4)**

Heaven is better than we can imagine it to be. **"But as it is written, Eye hath not seen, nor ear heard, neither have entered into the heart of man, the things which God hath prepared for them that love him." (1 Corinthians 2:9)**

The Holy Spirit

The Holy Spirit is the same Spirit who raised up Jesus from the dead. And he does many wonderful things for us. He baptizes us into the body of believers. He seals us until the day of redemption. He gives us hearts full of love for God and man. He gives us the desire to please God. And he empowers us to fulfill that desire.

The Holy Spirit is the Comforter that Jesus promised us. He helps us and he strengthens us. **"If you love me, keep my commandments, and I will pray the Father, and he shall give you another Comforter, that he may abide with you forever; even the Spirit of Truth; whom the world cannot receive, because it seeth him not, neither knoweth him: but ye shall know him; for he dwelleth with you, and shall be in you." (John 14:15-17)**

Jesus told his disciples to tarry in Jerusalem until they received the promise of the Father. And then, they would be endued with power from on high. On the Day of Pentecost, the Holy Spirit descended from Heaven. And he appeared on the Disciples' heads as cloven tongues of fire.

Then, they spilled out into the streets of Jerusalem. And they spoke the word of God with great boldness. Peter's spirit-filled preaching had a powerful effect on the people. They asked Peter, "What shall we do?" **"Then Peter said unto them, Repent, and be baptized every one of you in the name of Jesus Christ for the remission of sins, and ye shall receive the gift of the Holy Ghost." (Acts 2:38)**

The Holy Spirit is God's down payment that assures us his promises are true. **"He put his mark on us to show us that we are his, and he put his Spirit in our hearts to be a guarantee for all he has promised." (2 Corinthians 1:22 NCV)**

When you put your faith in Jesus, the Holy Spirit gives you spiritual life. And then, you're "in the Spirit." **"So then they that are in the flesh cannot please God. But ye are not in the flesh, but in the Spirit, if so be that the Spirit of God dwell in you. . . . But if the Spirit of him that raised up Jesus from the dead dwell in you, he that raised up Christ from the dead shall also quicken your mortal bodies by his Spirit that dwelleth in you." (Romans 8:8-9, 11)**

Jesus is the last Adam and he is a life-giving Spirit. **"And so it is written, the first man Adam was made a living soul; the last Adam was made a quickening spirit." (2 Corinthians 15:45)**

The Bible says that Jesus and the Holy Spirit are one and the same. **"Now the Lord is the Spirit, and where the Spirit of the Lord is, there is freedom. And we all, with unveiled face, beholding the glory of the Lord, are being transformed into the same image from one degree of glory to another. For this comes from the Lord who is the Spirit." (2 Corinthians 3:17-18 ESV)**

Inheritance

When you're in Christ, you're a child of God and a joint-heir with Jesus. **"The Spirit itself beareth witness with our spirit, that we are the children of God: and if children, then heirs; heirs of God, and joint-heirs with Christ; . . ." (Romans 8:16-17)**

Every born-again believer in Christ has an inheritance in heaven. **"Blessed be the God and Father of our Lord Jesus Christ, which according to his abundant mercy hath begotten us again unto a lively hope by the resurrection of Jesus Christ from the dead, to an inheritance incorruptible, and undefiled, and that fadeth not away, reserved in heaven for you, who are kept by the power of God through faith unto salvation ready to be revealed in the last time." (1 Peter 1:3-5)**

Paul reminded the Corinthians that they used to be unrighteous. But the Holy Spirit sanctified them. That means he cleaned them up on the inside. He changed their desires. And then, they changed their ways. **"Know ye not that the unrighteous shall not inherit the kingdom of God? Be not deceived: neither fornicators, nor idolaters, nor adulterers, nor effeminate, nor abusers of themselves with mankind, nor thieves, nor covetous, nor drunkards, nor revilers, nor extortioners, shall inherit the kingdom of God.**

And such were some of you: but ye are washed, but ye are sanctified, but ye are justified in the name of the Lord Jesus, and by the Spirit of our God." (1 Corinthians 6:9-11)

When you do what's right, the Lord will reward you. **"Servants, obey in all things your masters according to the flesh; not with eyeservice, as menpleasers; but in singleness of heart, fearing God; and whatsoever ye do, do it heartily, as to the Lord, and not unto men; knowing that of the Lord ye shall receive the**

reward of the inheritance: for ye serve the Lord Christ. But he that doeth wrong shall receive for the wrong which he hath done: and there is no respect of persons." (Colossians 3:22-25)

It takes faith and endurance to inherit the promises of God. You have to do what God says before you can receive what he's promised. **"For God is not unrighteous to forget your work and labor of love, which ye have shown toward his name, in that ye have ministered to the saints, and do minister. And we desire that every one of you do show the same diligence to the full assurance of hope unto the end: that ye be not slothful, but followers of them who through faith and patience inherit the promises."** (Hebrews 6:10-12)

Judgment

God sees everything that we do. And he requires us to do what's right. **"Fear God, and keep his commandments: for this is the whole duty of man. For God shall bring every work into judgment, with every secret thing, whether it be good, or whether it be evil." (Ecclesiastes 12:13-14)**

The Lord knows your thoughts and your intentions. And your actions determine the circumstances of your life. **"I the Lord search the heart and test the mind, to give to every man according to his ways, according to the fruit of his deeds." (Jeremiah 7:10 ESV)**

In your heart, you know what's right. So always do what's right. That's God's perfect law of liberty. **"So speak ye, and so do, as they that shall be judged by the law of liberty." (James 2:12)**

God treats you the same way that you treat others. **"Be ye therefore merciful, as your Father also is merciful. Judge not, and ye shall not be judged: condemn not, and ye shall not be condemned: forgive, and ye shall be forgiven:**

Give, and it shall be given unto you; good measure, pressed down, and shaken together, and running over, shall men give unto your bosom. For with the same measure that ye mete withal it shall be measured to you again." (Luke 6:36-37)

If you judge others, then God will judge you. And he will judge you to the same extent that you judged them. **"Don't judge others, or you will be judged. You will be judged in the same way that you judge others, and the amount you give to others will be given to you. (Matthew 7:1-2 NCV)**

God doesn't want us to punish the people who hurt us. **"Say not, I will do to him as he hath** done to me: I will render to the man according to his work." (Proverbs 24:29)

God doesn't want us to retaliate against anyone. He will repay them for their evil deeds. **"Repay no one evil for evil, but give thought to do what is honorable in the sight of all. . . . Beloved, never avenge yourselves, but leave it to the wrath of God, for it is written, Vengeance is mine, I will repay, says the Lord." (Romans 12:17, 19 ESV)**

Every sin has a built-in penalty. So nobody ever really gets away with anything. **"Be not deceived, God is not mocked, for whatsoever a man soweth, that shall he also reap." (Galatians 6:7)**

We will all stand before the judgment seat of Christ and be judged by him. **"For we must all appear before the judgment seat of Christ; that every one may receive the things done in his body, according to that he hath done, whether it be good or bad." (2 Corinthians 5:10)**

Justification

When we put our faith in Jesus, God declares us to be righteous. That's called justification. And it's the only thing that keeps us from going to Hell. **"Therefore being justified by faith, we have peace with God through our Lord Jesus Christ, by whom also we have access by faith into this grace in which we stand, and rejoice in hope of the glory of God." (Romans 5:1-2)**

Our justification is based on faith alone because God counts our faith as righteousness. **"Therefore by the deeds of the law there shall no flesh be justified in his sight: for by the law is the knowledge of sin. But now the righteousness of God without the law is manifested, being witnessed by the law and the prophets: even the righteousness of God which is by faith of Jesus Christ unto all and upon all them that believe: for there is no difference:**

For all have sinned, and come short of the glory of God; Being justified freely by his grace through the redemption that is in Christ Jesus:" (Romans 3:20-24)

We are saved by grace and grace is the unmerited favor of God. "For what saith the scripture? Abraham believed God, and it was counted unto him for righteousness. Now to him that worketh is the reward not reckoned of grace, but of debt. But to him that worketh not, but believeth on him that justifieth the ungodly, his faith is counted for righteousness." (Romans 4:3-5)

We are justified by our faith in Jesus and not by the works of the law. "Knowing that a man is not justified by the works of the law, but by the faith of Jesus Christ, even we have believed in Jesus Christ, that we might be justified by the faith of Christ, and not by the works of the law: for by the works of the law shall no flesh be justified." (Galatians 2:16)

God justifies everyone who believes on his Son Jesus. **"By him all that believe are justified from all things, from which ye could not be justified by the law of Moses." (Acts 13:39)**

The Kingdom of God

John the Baptist was the last of the Old Testament prophets. And he was the forerunner of Jesus. He told the people to repent because the Kingdom of God was at hand. **"The law and the prophets were until John: since that time the kingdom of God is preached, and every man presseth into it." (Luke 16:16)**

The Jews expected the Kingdom of God to be a material, earthly kingdom. But it's a spiritual kingdom that's not of this world. **"Giving thanks unto the Father, which hath made us meet to be partakers of the inheritance of the saints in light: who hath delivered us from the power of darkness, and hath translated us into the Kingdom of his dear Son:" (Colossians 1:12-13)**

You must be born again in order to enter the Kingdom of God. **"Jesus answered and said unto him, Verily, verily, I say unto thee, Except a man be born again, he cannot see the kingdom of God." (John 3:3)**

People who are spiritually dead can't understand the Kingdom of God. **"But the natural man receiveth not the things of the Spirit of God: for they are foolishness unto him: neither can he know them, because they are spiritually discerned." (1 Corinthians 2:14)**

Jesus told his disciples why he taught in parables. **"And he said unto them, Unto you it is given to know the mystery of the kingdom of God: but to them which are without, all these things are done in parables: That seeing they may see, and not perceive; and hearing they may hear, and not understand." (Mark 4:11-12)**

If you make God's Kingdom your highest priority, then the Lord will provide for all of your material needs. **"Therefore take no thought,** saying, What shall we eat? or, What shall we drink? or, Wherewithal shall we be clothed? (For after all these things do the Gentiles seek) for your heavenly Father knoweth that ye have need of all these things. But seek ye first the kingdom of God, and his righteousness; and all these things shall be added unto you." (Matthew 6:31-33)

Jesus repays us for the things we give up to follow him. **"Then Peter began to say unto him, Lo, we have left all, and have followed thee. And Jesus answered and said, Verily I say unto you, There is no man that hath left house, or brethren, or sisters, or father, or mother, or wife, or children, or lands, for my sake, and the gospel's,**

But he shall receive an hundredfold now in this time, houses and brethren, and sisters, and mothers, and children, and lands, with persecutions; and in the world to come eternal life." (Mark 10:28-30)

When Paul was under house arrest in Rome, many people came to hear him preach. And he taught them about the Kingdom of God. **"But we desire to hear of thee what thou thinkest: for as concerning this sect, we know that everywhere it is spoken against. And when they had appointed him a day, there came many to him into his lodging; to whom he expounded and testified the kingdom of God, persuading them concerning Jesus, both out of the law of Moses, and out of the prophets, from morning till evening. And some believed the things which were spoken, and some believed not." (Acts 28:22-24)**

The Lamb of God

God made a way for his people to escape the last Egyptian plague, the death of the firstborn. By faith, God's people applied lamb's blood to their doorposts. And the Death Angel "passed over" the houses where he saw the blood. That blood stood for the blood of Jesus, the Lamb of God, who died so that we can live.

John the Baptist was the first to recognize that Jesus is the Lamb of God. **"The next day John seeth Jesus coming unto him, and saith, Behold the Lamb of God, which taketh away the sin of the world." (John 1:29)**

Lambs that were sacrificed to God had to be perfect, without spot or blemish. Jesus was spiritually perfect because he was completely without sin. **"And if you call on the Father, who without respect of persons judgeth according** to every man's work, pass the time of your sojourning here in fear: Forasmuch as ye know that ye were not redeemed with corruptible things, as silver and gold, from your vain conversation received by tradition from your fathers; But with the precious blood of Christ, as of a lamb without blemish and without spot:" (1 Peter 1:17-19)

The Apostle John had a vision of heaven. And this is what he saw: **"And I beheld, and I heard the voice of many angels round about the throne and the beasts and the elders: and the number of them was ten thousand times ten thousand, and thousands of thousands; saying with a loud voice, Worthy is the Lamb that was slain to receive power, and riches, and wisdom and strength, and honor, and glory, and blessing."** (Revelation 5:11-12)

The Law

The law is the body of God's commandments and statutes recorded by Moses in the first five books of the Bible. This Psalm describes the man who delights in the law of the Lord and meditates on it day and night.

"But his delight is in the law of the Lord; and in his law doth he meditate day and night. And he shall be like a tree planted by the rivers of water, that bringeth forth his fruit in his season; his leaf also shall not wither; and whatsoever he doeth shall prosper." (Psalm 1:2-3)

King David advised his son Solomon to obey the law, so he would prosper in everything that he did. **"Now the days of David drew nigh that he should die; and he charged Solomon his son,**

saying, I go the way of all the earth: be thou strong therefore, and shew thyself a man;

And keep the charge of the Lord thy God, to walk in his ways, to keep his statutes, and his commandments, and his judgments, and his testimonies, as it is written in the law of Moses, that thou mayest prosper in all that thou doest, and whithersoever thou turnest thyself:" (1 Kings 2:1-3)

The law is God's perfect standard of righteousness. And it's impossible for us to meet that standard. That's why we need Jesus to save us. **"Wherefore the law was our schoolmaster to bring us unto Christ, that we might be justified by faith. But after that faith is come, we are no longer under a schoolmaster: for ye are all the children of God by faith in Christ Jesus."** (Galatians 3:24-26)

When you're in Christ, you're under God's perfect law of liberty instead of the law of sin and death. **"Knowing this, that the law is not made for a righteous man, but for the lawless and**

disobedient, for the ungodly and for sinners, for unholy and profane, for murderers of fathers and murderers of mothers, for manslayers, for whoremongers, for them that defile themselves with mankind, for menstealers, for liars, for perjured persons, and if there be any other thing that is contrary to sound doctrine; according to the glorious gospel of the blessed God, which was committed to my trust." (1 Timothy 1:9-11)

The scribes and the Pharisees thought they could save themselves by keeping the letter of the law. But salvation is through faith in Christ alone. And when we're loving our neighbors as ourselves, we're fulfilling the spirit of the law. **"For, brethren, ye have been called unto liberty; only use not liberty for an occasion to the flesh, but by love serve one another. For all the law is fulfilled in one word, even in this; thou shalt love thy neighbor as thyself." (Galatians 5:13-14)**

The Living Word of God

Jesus is the Living Word of God and he created all things. **"In the beginning was the Word, and the Word was with God, and the Word was God. The same was in the beginning with God. All things were made by him; and without him was not any thing made that was made." (John 1:1-3)**

Jesus sees everything that we do. And he knows everything that we think. **"For the word of God is quick and powerful, and sharper than any two-edged sword, piercing even to the dividing asunder of soul and spirit, and of the joints and marrow, and is a discerner of the thoughts and intents of the heart. Neither is there any creature that is not manifest in his sight: but all things are naked and opened unto the eyes of him with whom we have to do." (Hebrews 4:12-13)**

The Bible says that Peter, James and John saw Jesus in his glory on the Mount of Transfiguration. They said that his face shone like the sun and his clothing was as white as light. **"And the Word was made flesh, and dwelt among us, (and we beheld his glory, the glory as of the only begotten of the Father,) full of grace and truth." (John 1:14)**

John saw a vision of Jesus at the end of the age. And this is what he saw: **"And I saw heaven opened, and behold a white horse; and he that sat upon him was called Faithful and True, and in righteousness he doth judge and make war. His eyes were as a flame of fire, and on his head were many crowns; and he had a name written, that no man knew, but he himself. And he was clothed with a vesture dipped in blood: and his name is called The Word of God." (Revelation 19:11-13)**

Marriage

This is Jesus' definition of marriage: **"But from the beginning of the creation God made them male and female. For this cause shall a man leave his father and mother, and cleave to his wife; and they twain shall be one flesh: so then they are no more twain, but one flesh. What therefore God hath joined together, let not man put asunder." (Mark 10:6-9)**

The purpose of marriage is to produce godly children. **"Did he not make them one, with a portion of the Spirit in their union? And what was the one God seeking? Godly offspring. So guard yourself in your spirit, and let none of you be faithless to the wife of your youth." (Malachi 2:15 ESV)**

The Bible says that husbands and wives are one body and one spirit. **"God made husbands** and wives to become one body and one spirit for his purpose---so they would have children who are true to God. So be careful, and do not break your promise to the wife you married when you were young." (Malachi 2:15 NCV)

The Bible also says that Christians are one spirit with the Lord. **"But he who is joined to the Lord becomes one spirit with him." (1 Corinthians 6:17 NCV)**

Marriage is a picture of the relationship between Jesus and his church. **"Husbands, love your wives, even as Christ also loved the church, and gave himself for it; That he might sanctify and cleanse it with the washing of water by the word, That he might present to himself a glorious church, not having spot, or wrinkle, or any such thing; but that it should be holy and without blemish.**

So ought men to love their wives as their own bodies. He that loveth his wife loveth himself. For no man ever yet hated his own flesh; but nourisheth and cherished it, even as

the Lord the church: For we are members of his body, of his flesh, and of his bones.

For this cause shall a man leave his father and mother, and shall be joined unto his wife, and they two shall be one flesh. This is a great mystery: but I speak concerning Christ and the church. Nevertheless let every one of you in particular so love his wife even as himself; and the wife see that she reverence her husband." (Ephesians 5:25-33)

Jesus loves us unconditionally. He overlooks all of our shortcomings and he forgives them. And he wants husbands to do the same for their wives. **"Likewise, ye husbands, dwell with them, according to knowledge, giving honour to the wife as the weaker vessel, and as heirs together of the grace of life; that your prayers be not hindered." (1 Peter 3:7)**

Marriage is like a threefold cord. One strand of the cord is the husband's relationship with the Lord. Another strand is the wife's relationship with him. And the third strand is their relationship with each other. One of these strands might fail, or even two. But all three won't fail at the same time.

"Two are better than one; because they have a good reward for their labor. For if they fall, the one will lift up his fellow: but woe to him that is alone when he falleth; for he hath not another to help him up. Again, if two lie together, then they have heat: but how can one be warm alone? And if one prevail against him, two shall withstand him; and a threefold cord is not quickly broken." (Ecclesiastes 4:9-12)

The New Birth

The Holy Spirit raises us up from spiritual death and gives us spiritual life. He brings us into the Kingdom of God and makes us part of God's family. And that's what we call the new birth. **"Blessed be the God and Father of our Lord Jesus Christ! According to his great mercy, he has caused us to be born again to a living hope through the resurrection of Jesus Christ from the dead," (1 Peter 1:3 ESV)**

If you've been born born again by the Spirit of God, then you will live with the Lord forever. **"Being born again, not of corruptible seed, but of incorruptible, by the word of God, which liveth and abideth for ever." (1 Peter 1:23)**

Nicodemus was a religious leader who came to learn from Jesus. And Jesus told him about the new birth. **"Jesus answered and said unto him, Verily, verily, I say unto thee, except a man be born again, he cannot see the kingdom of God. Nicodemus saith unto him, How can a man be born when he is old? Can he enter the second time into his mother's womb, and be born?**

Jesus answered, Verily, verily, I say unto thee, except a man be born of water and of the Spirit, he cannot enter into the kingdom of God. That which is born of the flesh is flesh; and that which is born of the Spirit is spirit. Marvel not that I said unto thee, Ye must be born again." (John 3:3-7)

When you believe in Jesus, the Holy Spirit bears witness with your spirit that you've been born again. **"Whosoever believeth that Jesus is the Christ is born of God: and every one that loveth him that begat loveth him also that is begotten of him. . . .**

For whatsoever is born of God overcometh the world: and this is the victory that overcometh the world, even our faith. Who is he that overcometh the world, but he that believeth that Jesus is the Son of God? This is he that came by water and blood, even Jesus Christ; not by water only, but by water and blood.

And it is the Spirit that beareth witness, because the Spirit is truth. For there are three that bear record in heaven, the Father, the Word, and the Holy Ghost: and these three are one. And there are three that bear witness in earth, the spirit, and the water, and the blood: and these three agree in one. If we receive the witness of men, the witness of God is greater: for this is the witness of God which he hath testified of his Son." (1 John 5:1, 4-9)

The New Covenant

Speaking through his prophets Ezekiel and Jeremiah, God promised that he would make a new covenant with his people. He said that he would walk in us and write his laws upon our hearts. And that he would be our God and we would be his people.

"Behold, the days come, saith the Lord, that I will make a new covenant with the house of Israel, and with the house of Judah: not according to the covenant that I made with their fathers in the day that I took them by the hand to bring them out of the land of Egypt; which my covenant they brake, although I was an husband unto them, saith the Lord: but this shall be the covenant that I will make with the house of Israel; After those days, saith the Lord, I will put my law in their inward parts, and write it in their hearts; and will be their

God, and they shall be my people." (Jeremiah 31:31-33)

Jesus is the living fulfillment of that promise. He established the New Covenant by living a sinless life, by dying for our sins and rising from the dead. **"Then said he, Lo, I come to do thy will, O God. He taketh away the first, that he may establish the second. By the which will we are sanctified through the offering of the body of Jesus Christ once for all.**

And every priest standeth daily ministering and offering oftentimes the same sacrifices, which can never take away sins: But this man, after he had offered one sacrifice for sins for ever, sat down on the right hand of God; From henceforth expecting till his enemies be made his footstool. For by one offering he hath perfected for ever them that are sanctified." (Hebrews 10:9-14)

The New Covenant is better than the Old Covenant, because it's based on better promises. And because Jesus is the mediator of it. **"But now** hath he obtained a more excellent ministry, by how much also he is the mediator of a better covenant, which was established upon better promises. For if that first covenant had been faultless, then should no place have been sought for the second." (Hebrews 8:6-7)

Under the New Covenant, God forgives our sins and he also forgets about them. **"For I will be merciful to their unrighteousness, and their sins and their iniquities will I remember no more. In that he saith, a new covenant, he hath made the first old. Now that which decayeth and waxeth old is ready to vanish away." (Hebrews 8:12-13)**

Under the New Covenant, we're not merely observing the letter of the law outwardly. We're obeying the spirit of the law inwardly from our hearts. **"Forasmuch as ye are manifestly declared to be the epistle of Christ ministered by us, written not with ink, but with the Spirit of the living God; not in tables of stone, but in fleshy tables of the heart. . . .**

Who also hath made us able ministers of the new testament; not of the letter, but of the spirit: for the letter killeth, but the spirit giveth life." (2 Corinthians 3:3, 6)

Our High Priest

Jesus is our High Priest. And he knows what it's like to be human. He understands the temptations we face. And he knows that we're weak. He's already offered the perfect sacrifice for our sins. And now, he's sitting at the right hand of the Father where he's constantly interceding for us before him.

Jesus is our advocate before God. And his priesthood will continue forever. **"And they truly were many priests, because they were not suffered to continue by reason of death: But this man, because he continueth ever, hath an unchangeable priesthood. Wherefore he is able also to save them to the uttermost that come unto God by him, seeing he ever liveth to make intercession for them." (Hebrews 7:23-25)**

The Bible tells us to come boldly to the throne of God to obtain mercy and grace. **"Seeing then that we have a great high priest, that is passed into the heavens, Jesus the Son of God, let us hold fast our profession.**

For we have not an high priest which cannot be touched with the feeling of our infirmities; but was in all points tempted like as we are, yet without sin. Let us therefore come boldly unto the throne of grace, that we may obtain mercy, and find grace to help in time of need." (Hebrews 4:14-16)

Recompense

Recompense is payback. We're recompensed for everything that we do, both the good and the bad. The Bible says, **"Be not deceived; God is not mocked: for whatsoever a man soweth, that shall he also reap."** (Galatians 6:7)

The Lord knows our thoughts and our intentions. And the condition of our hearts determines what we receive from him. **"The heart is deceitful above all things, and desperately wicked: who can know it? I the Lord search the heart, I try the reins, even to give every man according to his ways, and according to the fruit of his doings."** (Jeremiah 17:9-10)

Our behavior determines the circumstances of our lives. **"For the work of a man shall he render unto him, and cause every man to find according to his ways. Yea, surely God will not do wickedly, neither will the Almighty pervert judgment." (Job 34:11-12)

God's word is righteousness. So when you're doing what the Bible says, you're doing righteousness. And the Lord will reward you for it. **"The Lord rewarded me according to my righteousness; according to the cleanness of my hands hath he recompensed me. For I have kept the ways of the Lord, and have not wickedly departed from my God." (2 Samuel 22:21-22)**

When you do what's right, the Lord will reward you for it. And he will repay the wicked for their evil deeds. **"Behold, the righteous shall be recompensed in the earth: much more the wicked and the sinner." (Proverbs 11:31)**

Everyone is recompensed for the evil that they do. **"There will be tribulation and distress for every human being who does evil, the Jew first and also to the Greek, but glory and honor and peace for everyone who does good, the Jew first and also the Greek. For God shows no partiality." (Romans 2:9-11 ESV)**

Redemption

Redemption is recovering something that's lost. When Adam rebelled against God, the whole human race was lost to Satan. But Jesus, the Second Adam, redeemed us from him. **"Let the redeemed of the Lord say so, whom he hath redeemed from the hand of the enemy." (Psalm 107:2)**

Jesus redeemed us from the curse of the law. **"Christ hath redeemed us from the curse of the law, being made a curse for us: for it is written, cursed is every one that hangeth on a tree: that the blessing of Abraham might come on the Gentiles through Jesus Christ; that we might receive the promise of the Spirit through faith." (Galatians 3:13-14)**

Jesus redeemed us with his blood. **"And if ye call on the Father, who without respect of** persons judgeth according to every man's work, pass the time of your sojourning here in fear: forasmuch as ye know that ye were not redeemed with corruptible things, as silver and gold, from your vain conversation received by tradition from your fathers; but with the precious blood of Christ, as of a lamb without blemish and without spot:" (1 Peter 1:17-19)

Jesus watches over us and he preserves our lives because we belong to him. "**But now thus saith the Lord that created thee, O Jacob, and he that formed thee, O Israel, Fear not: for I have redeemed thee, I have called thee by thy name; thou art mine. When thou passest through the waters, I will be with thee; and through the rivers, they shall not overflow thee: when thou walkest through the fire, thou shalt not be burned; neither shall the flame kindle upon thee." (Isaiah 43:1-2)**

The Righteousness of Christ

Even though God's promises defied logic, Abraham believed them anyway. He accepted God's word as the truth. And God substituted what Abraham had (faith) for something he could never earn (righteousness.) That is "the righteousness that is by faith." **"For what saith the scripture? Abraham believed God, and it was counted unto him for righteousness." (Romans 4:3)**

When you put your faith in Jesus, God counts your faith as righteousness too. **"For the promise, that he should be the heir of the world, was not to Abraham, or to his seed, through the law, but through the righteousness of faith. . . .**

Therefore it is of faith, that it might be by grace; to the end the promise might be sure to

all the seed; not to that only which is of the law, but to that also which is of the faith of Abraham; who is the father of us all." (Romans 4:13, 16)

If you believe that God's word is true, then you're going to act like you believe it. That's the kind of faith that God counts as righteousness. **"Even as Abraham believed God, and it was accounted to him for righteousness. Know ye therefore that they which are of faith, the same are the children of Abraham." (Galatians 3:6-7)**

When you were a sinner, you were free from righteousness. And now that God has declared you to be righteous, you're free from the power of sin. **"What then? Shall we sin because we are not under the law, but under grace? God forbid. Know ye not that whom ye yield yourselves servants to obey, his servants ye are to whom ye obey; whether of sin unto death, or to obedience unto righteousness?. . .**

For when ye were the servants of sin, ye were free from righteousness. What fruit had ye in those things whereof ye are now ashamed? For the end of those things is death. But now being made free from sin, and become servants of God, ye have your fruit unto holiness, and the end eternal life. For the wages of sin is death but the gift of God is eternal life through Jesus Christ our Lord." (Romans 6:15-16, 20-23)

Your salvation is based entirely on the righteousness of Jesus Christ. **"And be found in him, not having mine own righteousness, which is of the law, but that which is through the faith of Christ, the righteousness which is of God by faith:" (Philippians 3:9)**

Salvation

God loves us so much that he sent his Son Jesus to save us. And Jesus died for us so that we can live with him forever. **"For God so loved the world, that he gave his only begotten Son, that whosoever believeth in him should not perish, but have everlasting life. For God sent not his Son into the world to condemn the world; but that the world through him might be saved.**

He that believeth on him is not condemned: but he that believeth not is condemned already, because he hath not believed in the name of the only begotten Son of God." (John 3:16-18)

When you put your faith in Jesus, he comes to live in your heart. He changes you from the inside out. And then, your words and your deeds become your confession of faith in him.

"That if thou shalt confess with thy mouth the Lord Jesus, and shalt believe in thine heart that God hath raised him from the dead, thou shalt be saved. For with the heart man believeth unto righteousness; and with the mouth confession is made unto salvation." (Romans 10:9-10)

Most people think they have to work to earn their own salvation. But that's not true. The Bible says: **"Not by works of righteousness which we have done, but according to his mercy he saved us, by the washing of regeneration, and renewing of the Holy Ghost;" (Titus 3:5)**

The Bible says that salvation is a free gift. And that we don't have to do anything to earn it or deserve it. **"For by grace are ye saved through faith; and that not of yourselves; it is the gift of God: Not of works, lest any man should boast." (Ephesians 2:8-9)**

Our salvation is based entirely on Jesus' completed work on the cross. Our good works don't add anything to our salvation. But God does reward us for them. **"For other foundation can no man lay than that is laid, which is Jesus Christ. Now if any man build upon this foundation gold, silver, precious stones, wood, hay, stubble;**

Every man's work shall be made manifest: for the day shall declare it, because it shall be revealed by fire; and the fire shall try every man's work of which sort it is.

If any man's work abide which he hath build thereupon, he shall receive a reward. If any man's work shall be burned, he shall suffer loss: but he himself shall be saved; yet so as by fire." (1 Corinthians 3:11-15)

Sonship

John the Baptist saw the Spirit of God come down from heaven and rest on Jesus. **"Then John said, I saw the Spirit come down from heaven in the form of a dove and rest on him. Until then I did not know who the Christ was. But the God who sent me to baptize with water told me. 'You will see the Spirit come down and rest on a man; he is the One who will baptize with the Holy Spirit.' I have seen this happen, and I tell you the truth: This man is the Son of God." (John 1:32-34 NCV)**

Jesus has given us the power to become sons of God. **"He was in the world, and the world was made by him, and the world knew him not. He came unto his own, and his own received him not. But as many as received him, to them gave he power to become the sons of God, even to them that believe on his name: which were born, not of blood, nor or the will of the flesh, nor of the will of man, but of God." (John 1:10-13)**

Jesus is the only begotten Son of God. And we're God's adopted sons. **"But when the fullness of the time was come, God sent forth his Son, made of a woman, made under the law, to redeem them that were under the law, that we might receive the adoption of sons.**

And because ye are sons, God hath sent forth the Spirit of his Son into your hearts, crying, Abba, Father. Wherefore thou art no more a servant, but a son; and if a son, then an heir of God through Christ." (Galatians 4:4-7)

The Lord wants us to act like the sons of God that we are. **"Do all things without murmurings and disputings: That ye may be blameless and harmless, the sons of God, without rebuke, in the midst of a crooked and perverse nation, among whom ye shine as lights in the world." (Philippians 2:14-15)**

When you're following the promptings of the Holy Spirit, you're acting like a son of God. **"For as many as are led by the Spirit of God, they are the sons of God. For ye have not received the spirit of bondage again to fear; but ye have received the Spirit of adoption, whereby we cry, Abba, Father. The Spirit itself beareth witness with our spirit, that we are the children of God." (Romans 8:14-16)**

God loves us. And the world hates us because we belong to him. **"Behold, what manner of love the Father hath bestowed upon us, that we should be called the sons of God: therefore the world knoweth us not, because it knew him not. Beloved, now are we the sons of God, and it doth not yet appear what we shall be: but we know that, when he shall appear, we shall be like him; for we shall see him as he is. And every man that hath this hope in him purifieth himself, even as he is pure." (1 John 3:1-3)**

We're predestinated to be conformed to the image of Jesus. **"For whom he did foreknow, he also did predestinate to be conformed to the image of his Son, that he might be the firstborn among many brethren." (Romans 8:29)**

The Spirit of Truth

Jesus said, if you continue in his word, you'll know the truth and the truth will make you free. Freedom is the state of not being imprisoned or enslaved. When you know the truth of God's word, you can tell the difference between the truth and a lie. You won't believe the Devil's lies anymore. And you'll be free from his manipulation and control.

"The world" is the hostile environment in which we live. It's built on a foundation of lies and deception. And it's controlled by Satan. We're in the world but we're not of the world. **"Ye are of God, little children, and have overcome them: because greater is he that is in you, than he that is in the world.**

They are of the world: therefore speak they of the world, and the world heareth them. We

are of God: he that knoweth God heareth us; he that is not of God heareth not us. Hereby know we the spirit of truth, and the spirit of error." (1 John 4:4-6)**

The people of the world are spiritually dead. And they can't understand the things of God. **"But the natural man receiveth not the things of God: for they are foolishness unto him: neither can he know them, because they are spiritually discerned." (2 Corinthians 2:14)**

The Holy Spirit is the Spirit of Truth that Jesus promised to give us. **"If ye love me keep my commandments, and I will pray the Father, and he shall give you another Comforter, that he may abide with you forever; even the Spirit of truth; whom the world cannot receive, because it seeth him not, neither knoweth him: but ye know him; for he dwelleth with you, and shall be in you." (John 14:15-17)**

The Holy Spirit teaches us the things of God. **"Howbeit when he, the Spirit of truth, is come, he will guide you into all truth: for he shall not** speak of himself; but whatsoever he shall hear, that shall he speak: and he will show you things to come. He shall glorify me: for he shall receive of mine, and shall show it unto you. All things that the Father hath are mine: therefore said I, that he shall take of mine, and shall show it unto you." (John 16:13-15)

The Holy Spirit teaches us the word of God. "But the Comforter, which is the Holy Ghost, whom the Father will send in my name, he shall teach you all things, and bring all things to your remembrance, whatsoever I have said unto you." (John 14:26)

Spiritual Bread

When the Israelites were in the desert, God fed them with manna. And today, he feeds us with spiritual manna. Our daily bread is the word of God. It's new and fresh every morning. And all we have to do is gather it.

Jesus is the Bread of Life. And we feed on him by walking in God's ways. **"And he humbled thee, and suffered thee to hunger, and fed thee with manna, which thou knewest not, neither did thy fathers know; that he might make thee know that man doth not live by bread only, but by every word that proceedeth out of the mouth of the Lord doth man live." (Deuteronomy 8:3)**

When Jesus was fasting, Satan used bread to tempt him to sin. Jesus responded by quoting what the Bible says about bread. He defeated Satan with the truth of God's word. **"And when the tempter came to him, he said, If thou be the Son of God, command that these stones be made bread. But he answered and said, It is written, Man shall not live by bread alone, but by every word that proceedeth out of the mouth of God." (Matthew 4:3-4)**

Jesus is the bread that came down from heaven. And we are living by faith in him. **"Then Jesus said unto them, Verily, verily I say unto you, Moses gave you not that bread from heaven; but my Father giveth you the true bread from heaven. For the bread of God is he which cometh down from heaven, and giveth life unto the world. Then said they unto him, Lord, evermore give us this bread. And Jesus said unto them, I am the bread of life: he that cometh to me shall never hunger; and he that believeth on me shall never thirst." (John 6:32-35)**

"Eating the Lord's flesh" and "drinking his blood" are metaphors. "Eating his flesh" is doing God's will. And "drinking his blood" is receiving the free gift of salvation. Jesus said, **"I am the**

living bread which came down from heaven: if any man eat of this bread, he shall live for ever: and the bread that I will give is my flesh, which I will give for the life of the world. . . . He that eateth my flesh, and drinketh my blood, dwelleth in me, and I in him." (John 6:51, 56)

The bread and the wine of the Lord's Supper represent Jesus' body and his blood. Discerning the Lord's body is applying God's word to our lives. And the wine reminds us that Jesus shed his blood for us.

"For I have received of the Lord that which also I delivered unto you, that the Lord Jesus, the same night in which he was betrayed took bread: and when he had given thanks, he brake it, and said, Take, eat: this is my body, which is broken for you: this do in remembrance of me.

After the same manner also he took the cup, when he had supped, saying, This cup is the new testament in my blood: this do ye, as oft as ye drink it, in remembrance of me. . . .

But let a man examine himself, and so let him eat of that bread, and drink of that cup. For he that eateth and drinketh unworthily, eateth and drinketh damnation to himself; not discerning the Lord's body. For this cause many are weak and sickly among you, and many sleep. For if we would judge ourselves, we should not be judged." (1 Corinthians 11:23-25, 28-31)

Spiritual Drink

God's word is as essential to our souls as water is to our bodies. A "broken cistern" is a man-made religion that's not based on the truth of God's word. **"For my people have committed two evils; they have forsaken me, the fountain of living waters, and hewed them out cisterns, broken cisterns, that can hold no water." (Jeremiah 2:13)**

The Holy Spirit is the living water that Jesus gives to everyone who believes on him. **"In the last day, that great day of the feast, Jesus stood and cried, saying, If any man thirst, let him come unto me, and drink. He that believeth on me, as the scripture hath said, out of his belly shall flow rivers of living water. (But this spake he of the Spirit, which they that believe on him should receive: for the Holy Ghost was not yet** given; because that Jesus was not yet glorified.)" (John 7:37-39)**

Jesus told the woman at the well about the living water that he provides. **"Jesus answered and said unto her, If thou knewest the gift of God, and who it is that saith to thee, Give me to drink; thou wouldest have asked of him, and he would have given thee living water. . . . But whosoever drinketh of the water that I shall give him shall never thirst; but the water that I shall give him shall be in him a well of water springing up into everlasting life." (John 4:10, 14)**

The Holy Spirit told Simon that Jesus is the Son of the Living God. And Jesus changed his name to Peter, which means "rock." Jesus built his church on this rock of revelation from the Holy Spirit, that he is the Son of God. Jesus told Peter, **"Blessed art thou, Simon Bar-Jona, for flesh and blood hath not revealed it unto thee, but my Father which is in heaven. And I say also unto thee, that thou art Peter, and upon this rock I will build my church; and the gates**

of hell shall not prevail against it." (Matthew 16:17-18)

The Israelites were baptized unto Moses. And they all drank from the same spiritual Rock. We're baptized into Jesus Christ. And we all drink from the same spiritual rock of revelation that Simon Peter did. **"Moreover, brethren, I would not that ye should be ignorant, how that all our fathers were under the cloud, and all passed through the sea; and were all baptized unto Moses in the cloud and in the sea; and did all eat the same spiritual meat; and did all drink the same spiritual drink: for they drank of that spiritual Rock that followed them: and that Rock was Christ." (1 Corinthians 10:1-4)**

Spiritual Meat

"Eating spiritual meat" is a metaphor for doing God's will. And it's God's will for us to love people---to have empathy for them and to treat them like we want to be treated. When we're doing this, we're pleasing God. And when we please God, he shows us his favor.

Jesus explained to his disciples that "eating meat" is doing God's will. **"In the meanwhile his disciples prayed him, saying, Master, eat. But he said unto them, I have meat to eat that ye know not of. Therefore said the disciples one to another, Hath any man brought of him aught to eat? Jesus said unto them, my meat is to do the will of him that sent me and to finish his work."** (John 4:31-34)

Doing God's will makes us grow up and become mature followers of Jesus. **"We have** much to say about this, but it is hard to explain because you are slow to learn. In fact, though by this time you ought to be teachers, you need someone to teach you the elementary truths of God's word all over again.

You need milk, not solid food! Anyone who lives on milk, being still an infant, is not acquainted with the teaching about righteousness. But solid food is for the mature, who by constant use have trained themselves to distinguish good from evil." (Hebrews 5:11-14)

It's God's will for you to believe on his Son Jesus Christ. **"Labor not for the meat that perisheth but for that meat which endureth unto everlasting life, which the Son of man shall give unto you: for him hath God the Father sealed. Then said they unto him, What shall we do, that we might work the works of God? Jesus answered and said unto them, This is the work of God, that ye believe on him whom he hath sent." (John 6:27-29)**

The Voice of God

God's voice is an internal voice. You hear it with your spiritual ears. And when the Lord speaks to you, you will know that it's him. Jesus said, **"My sheep hear my voice, and I know them, and they follow me:" (John 10:27)**

God gave Elijah a great victory over the prophets of Baal. But when Queen Jezebel threatened to kill him, he ran away and hid in a cave. He heard a great wind, an earthquake and a fire. But God's voice wasn't in those things. God spoke to Elijah in a "still small voice." And he speaks to us in the same "still small voice."

"And he said, Go forth, and stand upon the mount before the Lord. And, behold, the Lord passed by, and a great and strong wind rent the mountains, and brake in pieces the rocks before the Lord; but the Lord was not in the

wind: and after the wind an earthquake; but the Lord was not in the earthquake: and after the earthquake a fire; but the Lord was not in the fire: and after the fire a still small voice.

And it was so, when Elijah heard it, that he wrapped his face in his mantle and went out, and stood in the entering of the cave. And, behold, there came a voice unto him, and said, What doest thou here, Elijah?" (1 Kings 19:11-13)

You usually hear God's voice at night when you're quiet and still. Your "reins" are your conscience. **"I will bless the Lord, who hath given me counsel: my reins also instruct me in the night seasons." (Psalm 16:7)**

The Lord instructs you while you're asleep. **"For God speaketh once, yea twice, yet man perceiveth it not. In a dream, in a vision of the night, when deep sleep falleth upon men, in slumberings upon the bed; Then he openeth the ears of men, and sealeth their instruction, that he may withdraw man from his purpose,** and hide pride from man. He keepeth back his soul from the pit, and his life from perishing by the sword." (Job 33:14-18)

The Lord tells you which way to go. **"And thine ears shall hear a word behind thee, saying. This is the way, walk ye in it, when ye turn to the right hand, and when ye turn to the left." (Isaiah 30:21)**

Everything the Lord says is consistent with the Bible. That's how you recognize his voice. **"To him the porter openeth; and the sheep hear his voice: and he calleth his own sheep by name, and leadeth them out. And when he putteth forth his own sheep, he goeth before them, and the sheep follow him, for they know his voice. And a stranger will they not follow, but will flee from him: for they know not the voice of strangers." (John 10:3-5)**

The Lord never contradicts the Bible. We know that the Bible says, **"Thou shalt not kill." (Exodus 20:13)** So if a voice tells you to kill someone, that's not God's voice. The Bible says, **"God is not the author of confusion." (1 Corinthians 14:33)** So if a voice causes you to be confused, that's not God's voice.

The Bible says, **"God has not given us the spirit of fear." (2 Timothy 1:7)** So if a voice makes you afraid, that's not God's voice. The Bible says, **"God will speak peace unto his people." (Psalm 85:8)** So if a voice takes away your peace, that's not God's voice.

The Will of God

God's word and his will are the same. So when you're doing what the Bible says, you're doing the will of God. God is always looking out for your best interests. And his will always gives you the best possible outcome. So always do the will of God. And ask him for his will to be done in your life.

Jesus gave his disciples this model prayer that we call the Lord's Prayer. In this prayer, Jesus asks for God's will to be done. **"After this manner therefore pray ye: Our Father which art in heaven, Hallowed be thy name. Thy kingdom come. Thy will be done in earth, as it is in heaven. Give us this day our daily bread. And forgive us our debts, as we forgive our debtors. And lead us not into temptation, but deliver us from evil: For thine is the kingdom,** and the power, and the glory, for ever. Amen." (Matthew 6:9-13)

Jesus always does the will of God. And he wants us to do the same. **"Who in the days of his flesh, when he had offered up prayers and supplications with strong crying and tears unto him that was able to save him from death, and was heard in that he feared; though he were a Son, yet learned he obedience by the things which he suffered; and being made perfect, he became the author of eternal salvation unto all them that obey him." (Hebrews 5:7-9)**

The Bible renews our minds and it teaches us what the will of God is. **"And be not conformed to this world: but be ye transformed by the renewing of your mind, that ye may prove what is that good, and acceptable, and perfect, will of God." (Romans 12:2 ESV)**

It's God's will for everyone to be saved. But everyone doesn't know about God's free gift of salvation. And some people will not accept it. **"For this is good and acceptable in the sight of God our Savior; Who will have all men to be saved, and to come unto the knowledge of the truth." (1 Timothy 2:3-4)**

Wisdom

Wisdom is a mindset. It's knowing what God wants you to do. And doing your best to accomplish it. **"The fear of the Lord is the beginning of wisdom: a good understanding have all they that do his commandments." (Psalm 111:10)**

This is what God says about wisdom: **"Wisdom is the principal thing; therefore get wisdom: and with all thy getting get understanding. Exalt her, and she shall promote thee: she shall bring thee to honour, when thou dost embrace her. She shall give to thine head an ornament of grace: a crown of glory shall she deliver to thee.**

Hear, O my son, and receive my sayings; and the years of thy life shall be many. I have taught thee in the way of wisdom; I have led thee in right paths. When thou goest, thy steps

shall not be straitened; and when thou runnest, thou shalt not stumble. Take fast hold of instruction; let her not go: keep her; for she is thy life." (Proverbs 4:7-13)

The Lord also says, if you want to be happy, get wisdom. If you want to live a long life, get wisdom. And if you want to be rich, get wisdom.

"Happy is the man that findeth wisdom, and the man that getteth understanding: for the merchandise of it is better than the merchandise of silver, and the gain thereof than fine gold. She is more precious than rubies: and all the things thou canst desire are not to be compared unto her.

Length of days is in her right hand; and in her left hand riches and honor. Her ways are ways of pleasantness, and all her paths are peace. She is a tree of life to them that lay hold upon her: and happy is every one that retaineth her." (Proverbs 3:13-18)

Wisdom is a free gift from God. And we receive it by faith. **"If any of you lack wisdom,**

let him ask of God, that giveth to all men liberally, and upbraideth not; and it shall be given him. But let him ask in faith, nothing wavering. For he that wavereth is like a wave of the sea driven with the wind and tossed. For let not that man think that he shall receive any thing of the Lord." (James 1:5-7)

Jesus gives us wisdom and righteousness. He sanctifies us and he redeems us. **"But God hath chosen the foolish things of the world to confound the wise; and God hath chosen the weak things of the world to confound the things which are mighty; and base things of the world, and things which are despised, hath God chosen, yea, and things which are not, to bring to nought things that are: that no flesh should glory in his presence.**

But of him are ye in Christ Jesus, who of God is made unto us wisdom, and righteousness, and sanctification, and redemption: that according as it is written, He that glorieth, let him glory in the Lord." (1 Corinthians 1:27-31)

The Written Word of God

The Bible is the written word of God. It's all about Jesus, the Living Word of God. And it's God's instruction book for life. **"All scripture is given by inspiration of God, and is profitable for doctrine, for reproof, for correction, for instruction in righteousness: that the man of God may be perfect, thoroughly furnished unto all good works." (2 Timothy 3:16-17)**

Men may have written the Bible. But God told them what to say. **"Knowing this first, that no prophecy of the Bible is of any private interpretation. For the prophecy came not in old time by the will of man: but holy men of God spake as they were moved by the Holy Ghost." (2 Peter 1:20-21)**

These are God's instructions to you concerning the Bible: **"My son, attend to my** words; Let them not depart from thine eyes; keep them in the midst of thine heart. For they are life unto those that find them, and health to all their flesh. Keep thy heart with all diligence; for out of it are the issues of life." (Proverbs 4:20-23)

"My son, forgot not my law; but let thine heart keep my commandments: For length of days, and long life, and peace, shall they add to thee. Let not mercy and truth forsake thee: bind them about thy neck; write them upon the table of thine heart: So shalt thou find favour and good understanding in the sight of God and man." (Proverbs 3:1-4)

These were Paul's instructions to his protégé, the young preacher Timothy. And they're also God's instructions to you. **"But continue thou in the things which thou hast learned and hast been assured of, knowing of whom thou has learned them; And that from a child thou hast known the holy scriptures, which are able to make thee wise unto salvation through faith which is in Christ Jesus." (2 Timothy 3:14-15)**

"Meditate upon these things; give thyself wholly to them; that thy profiting may appear to all. Take heed unto thyself, and unto the doctrine; continue in them: for in doing this thou shalt both save thyself, and them that hear thee." (1 Timothy 4:15-16)

Paul told Timothy to preach the word of God, to preach the Bible. And every preacher of the Gospel ought to do the same. **"Preach the word; be instant in season, out of season; reprove, rebuke, exhort with all long-suffering and doctrine." (2 Timothy 4:2)**

When people hear the word of God, it causes faith to arise in their hearts. **"So then faith cometh by hearing, and hearing by the word of God." (Romans 10:17)**

Hearing God's word only benefits us when we act on it. **"But be doers of the word, and not hearers only, deceiving yourselves. For if anyone is a hearer of the word and not a doer, he is like a man who looks intently at his natural face in a mirror.**

For he looks at himself and goes away and at once forgets what he was like. But the one who looks into the perfect law of liberty, and perseveres, being no hearer that forgets but a doer who acts, he will be blessed in his doing." (James 1:22-25 ESV)

Your Personal Savior

Since you're descended from Adam, you're a natural born sinner. You've sinned and fallen short of the glory of God. And the wages of sin is death. But God sent his Son Jesus, the Second Adam, to save you from sin and death and Hell. And when you put your faith in him, he will come and live in you.

"But when the right time came, God sent his Son who was born of a woman and lived under the law. God did this so he could buy freedom for those who were under the law and so we could become his children. Since you are God's children, God sent the Spirit of his Son into your hearts, and the Spirit cries out, 'Father.' " (Galatians 4:4-6 NCV)

Jesus is uniquely qualified to be your Savior. He's the only begotten Son of God and the Second

Adam. He's the only man who ever lived a sinless life. He died for your sins and he gave you the benefit of his righteousness.

"Therefore as by the offense of one judgment came upon all men to condemnation; even so by the righteousness of one the free gift came upon all men unto justification of life. For as by one man's disobedience many were made sinners, so by the obedience of one shall many be made righteous." (Romans 5:18-19)

Jesus is the only true Savior of mankind. "Neither is there salvation in any other: for there is none other name under heaven given among men, whereby we must be saved." (Acts 4:12)

Jesus is the only way to the One True God. **"Jesus saith unto him, I am the way, the truth, and the life: no man cometh unto the Father, but by me." (John 14:6)**

12 Things You Need to Know

1. The Bible is the word of God and it is the truth. Men may have written it, but God told them what to say.

"Knowing this first, that no prophecy of the scripture is of any private interpretation. For the prophecy came not in old time by the will of man: but holy men of God spake as they were moved by the Holy Ghost." (2 Peter 1:20-21)

"All scripture is given by inspiration of God, and is profitable for doctrine, for reproof, for correction, for instruction in righteousness: that the man of God may be perfect, thoroughly furnished unto all good works." (2 Timothy 3:16-17)

"Then said Jesus to those Jews which believed on him, If ye continue in my word, then are ye my disciples indeed; And ye shall know the truth, and the truth shall make you free." (John 8:31-32)

2. God sent his Son Jesus to save us from sin and death and Hell.

"And as Moses lifted up the serpent in the wilderness, even so must the Son of man be lifted up: That whosoever believeth in him should not perish, but have eternal life. For God so loved the world, that he gave his only begotten Son, that whosoever believeth in him should not perish but have everlasting life. For God sent not his son into the world to condemn the world; but that the world through him might be saved." (John 3:14-17)

"The word is nigh thee, even in thy mouth, and in thy heart: that is, the word of faith, which we preach: That if thou shalt confess with thy mouth the Lord Jesus, and shalt believe in thine heart that God hath raised him from the dead, thou shalt be saved. For with the heart man believeth unto righteousness, and with the mouth confession is made unto salvation." (Romans 10:8-10)

3. Jesus is the only true Savior and the only way to the One True God.

"Let this mind be in you, which was also in Christ Jesus: Who, being in the form of God, thought it not robbery to be equal with God: But made himself of no reputation, and took upon him the form of a servant, and was made in the likeness of men: And being found in fashion as a man, he humbled himself, and became obedient unto death, even the death of the cross.

Wherefore God also hath highly exalted him, and given him a name which is above every name: That at the name of Jesus every knee should bow, of things in heaven, and things in earth, and things under the earth; And that every tongue should confess that Jesus Christ is Lord, to the glory of God the Father." (Philippians 2:5-11)

"Neither is there salvation in any other; for there is no other name under heaven given among men, whereby we must be saved." (Acts 4:12)

"Jesus saith unto him, I am the way, the truth, and the life: no man cometh to the Father but by me." (John 14:6)

"I am Alpha and Omega, the beginning and the ending, saith the Lord, which is, and which was, and which is to come, the Almighty. . . .

And when I saw him, I fell at his feet as dead. And he laid his right hand upon me, saying unto me, Fear not; I am the first and the last: I am he that liveth, and was dead; and, behold, I am alive for evermore, Amen; and have the keys of hell and of death." (Revelation 1:8, 17-18)

4. Salvation is a free gift from God. You don't have to earn it or deserve it. Grace is the unmerited favor of God. And you are saved by grace when you put your faith in Jesus.

"For by grace are ye saved through faith; and that not of yourselves, it is the gift of God: not of works, lest any man should boast." (Ephesians 2:8-9)

"Therefore it is of faith, that it might be by grace; to the end the promise might be sure to all the seed; not to that only which is of the law, but to that also which is of the faith of Abraham; who is the father of us all." (Romans 4:16)

"Not by works of righteousness which we have done, but according to his mercy he saved us, by the washing of regeneration, and renewing of the Holy Spirit, which he shed on us abundantly through Jesus Christ our Savior, that being justified by his grace, we should be made heirs according to the hope of eternal life." (Titus 3:5-7)

5. If you're a born-again believer in Jesus, then the Spirit of God lives in you.

"If a man love me, he will keep my words and my Father will love him, and we will come unto him, and make our abode with him." (John 14:21-23)

"Know ye not that ye are the temple of God, and that the Spirit of God dwelleth in you?" (1 Corinthians 3:16)

"And what agreement hath the temple of God with idols? For ye are the temple of the living God, as God hath said, I will dwell in them, and walk in them; and I will be their God, and they shall be my people." (2 Corinthians 6:16)

"I am crucified with Christ: nevertheless I live; Yet not I, but Christ liveth in me: and the life which I now live in the flesh I live by the faith of the Son of God, who loved me and gave himself for me." (Galatians 2:20)

6. If you're a born-again believer in Jesus, then you're a member of God's family. You're a

joint-heir with Jesus. You're on the way to Heaven and you have an inheritance there.

"Blessed be the God and Father of our Lord Jesus Christ! According to his great mercy, he has caused us to be born again to a living hope through the resurrection of Jesus Christ from the dead, to an inheritance that is imperishable, undefiled, and unfading, kept in heaven for you." (1 Peter 1:3-4 ESV)

"The Spirit itself beareth witness with our spirit, that we are the children of God: And if children, then heirs; heirs of God, and joint-heirs with Christ; if so be that we suffer with him, that we may be also glorified together. For I reckon that the sufferings of this present time are not worthy to be compared with the glory which shall be revealed in us." (Romans 8:16-18)

7. Jesus is the author and finisher of your faith. He gives you the desire to please God. And he empowers you to fulfill that desire.

"Wherefore seeing we also are compassed about with so great a cloud of witnesses, let us lay aside every weight, and the sin which doth so easily beset us, and let us run with patience the race that is set before us,

Looking unto Jesus the author and finisher of our faith; who for the joy that was set before him endured the cross, despising the shame, and is set down at the right hand of the throne of God." (Hebrews 12:1-2)

"Being confident of this very thing, that he which hath begun a good work in you will perform it until the day of Jesus Christ:" (Philippians 1:6)

"God is working in you to help you want to do and be able to do what pleases him." (Philippians 2:13 NCV)

8. When you're doing what the Bible says, you're doing righteousness. And while your righteousness doesn't add anything to your salvation, God does reward you for it.

"And it shall be our righteousness, if we observe to do all these commandments before the Lord our God, as he hath commanded us." (Deuteronomy 6:25)

"The Lord rewarded me according to my righteousness; according to the cleanness of my hands hath he recompensed me. For I have kept the ways of the Lord, and have not wickedly departed from my God." (2 Samuel 22:21-22)

"The Lord rewarded me because I did what was right, because I did what the Lord said was right." (Psalm 18:24 NCV)

"If people please God, God will give them wisdom, knowledge, and joy. But sinners will get only the work of gathering and storing wealth that they will have to give to the ones who please God. So all their work is useless, like chasing the wind." (Ecclesiastes 2:26 NCV)

9. When you're doing what's right, your conscience doesn't condemn you. And you have confidence toward God.

"My little children, let us not love in word, neither in tongue; but in deed and in truth. And hereby we know that we are of the truth, and shall assure our hearts before him. For if our heart condemn us, God is greater than our heart, and knoweth all things." (1 John 3:18-20)

"Beloved, if our heart condemn us not, then have we confidence toward God. And whatsoever we ask, we receive of him because we keep his commandments, and do those things that are pleasing in his sight." (1 John 3:21-22)

"Cast not away therefore your confidence, which hath great recompense of reward. For ye have need of patience, that, after ye have done the will of God, ye might receive the promise." (Hebrews 10:35-36)

"And this is the confidence that we have before him, that if we ask anything according to his will he heareth us. And we know that if he hears us, we know that we have the things we desired of him." (1 John 5:15)

10. Sin is showing a lack of love for others. It's the opposite of righteousness. And it keeps God from hearing our prayers.

"Now we know that God heareth not sinners: but if any man be a worshipper of God, and doeth his will, him he heareth." (John 9:31)

"If I had cherished iniquity in my heart, the Lord would not have listened to me." (Psalm 66:18 ESV)

"The eyes of the Lord are upon the righteous and his ears are open to their cry." (Psalm 34:15)

"For the eyes of the Lord run to and fro throughout the whole earth, to shew himself strong in the behalf of them whose heart is perfect toward him. . . . " (2 Chronicles 16:9)

11. When you confess your sins to God, he will forgive you for them. And he will also cleanse you from all unrighteousness.

"If we say that we have no sin, we deceive ourselves and the truth is not in us. If we confess our sins, he is faithful and just to forgive us our sins, and to cleanse us from all unrighteousness." (1 John 1:8-9)

"Let the wicked forsake his way, and the unrighteous man his thoughts: and let him return unto the Lord and he will have mercy upon him; and to our God, for he will abundantly pardon." (Isaiah 55:7)

"Come now, and let us reason together, saith the Lord: though your sins be as scarlet, they shall be white as snow; though they be red like crimson, they shall be as wool." (Isaiah 1:18)

12. Every man's judgment comes from God and God is just.

"Be not deceived, God is not mocked, for whatsoever a man soweth, that shall he also reap." (Galatians 6:7)

"I the Lord search the heart and test the mind, to give every man according to his ways, according to the fruit of his deeds." (Jeremiah 17:10 ESV)

"For the work of a man shall he render unto him, and cause every man to find according to his ways. Yea, surely God will not do wickedly, neither will the Almighty pervert judgment." (Job 34:11-12)

"Behold, the righteous shall be recompensed in the earth; much more, the wicked and the sinner." (Proverbs 11:31)

"He that doeth wrong shall receive for the wrong which he hath done: and there is no respect of persons." (Colossians 3:25)

Thank you for reading *A Crash Course in The Bible*. I hope that it helps you in your walk with the Lord.

Larry Vaughn

www.ingramcontent.com/pod-product-compliance
Lightning Source LLC
Chambersburg PA
CBHW070614010526
44118CB00012B/1505